The Calico Mother Goose Book of

Earth, Moon, and Sky

Illustrated by T. Lewis

A CALICO BOOK
Published by Contemporary Books, Inc.
CHICAGO • NEW YORK

Library of Congress Cataloging-in-Publication Data
Mother Goose. Selections.
The Calico Mother Goose book of earth, moon, and sky
illustrated by T. Lewis. p. cm.
Summary: Selected Mother Goose rhymes feature
various aspects of nature.
ISBN 0-8092-4394-6
1. Nursery rhymes. 2. Children's poetry.
[1. Nursery rhymes. 2. Nature—Poetry.]
I. Lewis, T. (Thomas), ill. II. Title.
PZ8.3.M85 1989c
398′.8—dc19
88-30199
CIP
AC

Quilting by Audrey Ackerman
Designed by Paul Leibowitz
Edited by Wendy Wax

Published by Contemporary Books, Inc.
180 North Michigan Avenue, Chicago, Illinois 60601
Manufactured in the United States of America
Library of Congress Catalog Card Number: 88-30199
International Standard Book Number: 0-8092-4394-6

Published simultaneously in Canada by Beaverbooks, Ltd.
195 Allstate Parkway, Valleywood Business Park
Markham, Ontario L3R 4T8 Canada

Contents

Introduction

Enter a pastoral world vastly different from the technological world of today, a world where Bo-peep spends her afternoon in a meadow looking for the tails of lost sheep while Boy Blue sleeps under the hay, where the wind blows to grind the miller's corn and an eency weency spider climbs a waterspout time and again, where a little star twinkles for wish making and an old woman sweeps cobwebs from the sky.

The perfect rhythms and rhymes of Mother Goose joyfully introduce children to the natural events of the earth and sky. What a wonderful way for small children to learn about the simpler lifestyles of an agrarian past, to learn to trust the vicissitudes of weather, and to blend fact with fantasy when confronting the vast mystery of space.

As the nursery rhymes in this collection are read and reread to small children, the world of nature will unfold as an enchanting arena for learning and discovery, because Mother Goose encourages an attitude of simple wonder—an attitude which no amount of modern technology will ever be able to change. For why *does* that little star twinkle in the night? What *will* poor Robin do when the North Wind blows? And will that eency weency spider *ever* get to the top of the waterspout?

Mary Pope Osborne

Boy Blue

Little Boy Blue, come blow your horn,
The sheep's in the meadow, the cow's in the corn.
Where is the boy who looks after the sheep?
He's under a haycock fast asleep.

Will you wake him? No, not I,
For if I do, he's sure to cry.

When Clouds Appear

When clouds appear
Like rocks and towers,
The earth's refreshed
By frequent showers.

Little Drops of Water

Little drops of water,
Little grains of sand,
Make the mighty ocean,
And the pleasant land.

Harvest

The boughs do shake and the bells do ring,
So merrily comes our harvest in,
Our harvest in, our harvest in,
So merrily comes our harvest in.

We've ploughed, we've sowed,
We've reaped, we've mowed,
We've got our harvest in.

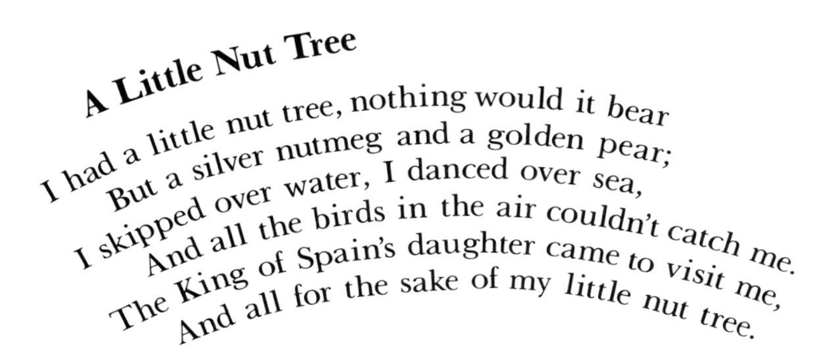

A Little Nut Tree

I had a little nut tree, nothing would it bear
But a silver nutmeg and a golden pear;
I skipped over water, I danced over sea,
And all the birds in the air couldn't catch me.
The King of Spain's daughter came to visit me,
And all for the sake of my little nut tree.

Little Bo-peep

Little Bo-peep has lost her sheep,
And doesn't know where to find them;
Leave them alone, and they'll come home,
Bringing their tails behind them.

Little Bo-peep fell fast asleep,
And dreamt she heard them bleating;
But when she awoke, she found it a joke,
For they were still a-fleeting.

Then she took her little crook,
Determined for to find them;
She found them indeed, but it made her heart bleed,
For they'd left their tails behind them.

It happened one day, as Bo-peep did stray
Into a meadow hard by,
There she espied their tails side by side,
All hung on a tree to dry.

She heaved a sigh, and wiped her eye,
And over the hillocks went rambling,
And tried what she could, as a shepherdess should,
To tack again each to its lambkin.

Star Light, Star Bright

Star light, star bright,
  First star I see tonight,
I wish I may, I wish I might,
  Have the wish I wish tonight.

Twinkle, Twinkle, Little Star

Twinkle, twinkle, little star,
How I wonder what you are!
Up above the world so high,
Like a diamond in the sky.

When the blazing sun is gone,
When he nothing shines upon,
Then you show your little light,
Twinkle, twinkle, all the night.

Then the traveler in the dark
Thanks you for your tiny spark:
How could he see where to go,
If you did not twinkle so?

In the dark blue sky you keep,
Often through my curtains peep,
For you never shut your eye,
Till the sun is in the sky.

As your bright and tiny spark
Lights the traveler in the dark,
Though I know not what you are,
Twinkle, twinkle, little star.

If All the World Was Paper

If all the world was paper,
And all the sea was ink,
If all the trees were bread and cheese,
What should we have to drink?

It's enough to make a man like me
Scratch his head and think.

The Man in the Wilderness

The man in the wilderness asked me
How many strawberries grew in the sea.
I answered him as I thought good,
As many as red herrings grew in the wood.

Eency Weency Spider

Eency weency spider climbed the water spout,

Down came the rain and washed the spider out,

Out came the sun and dried up all the rain,

Now eency weency spider went up the spout again.

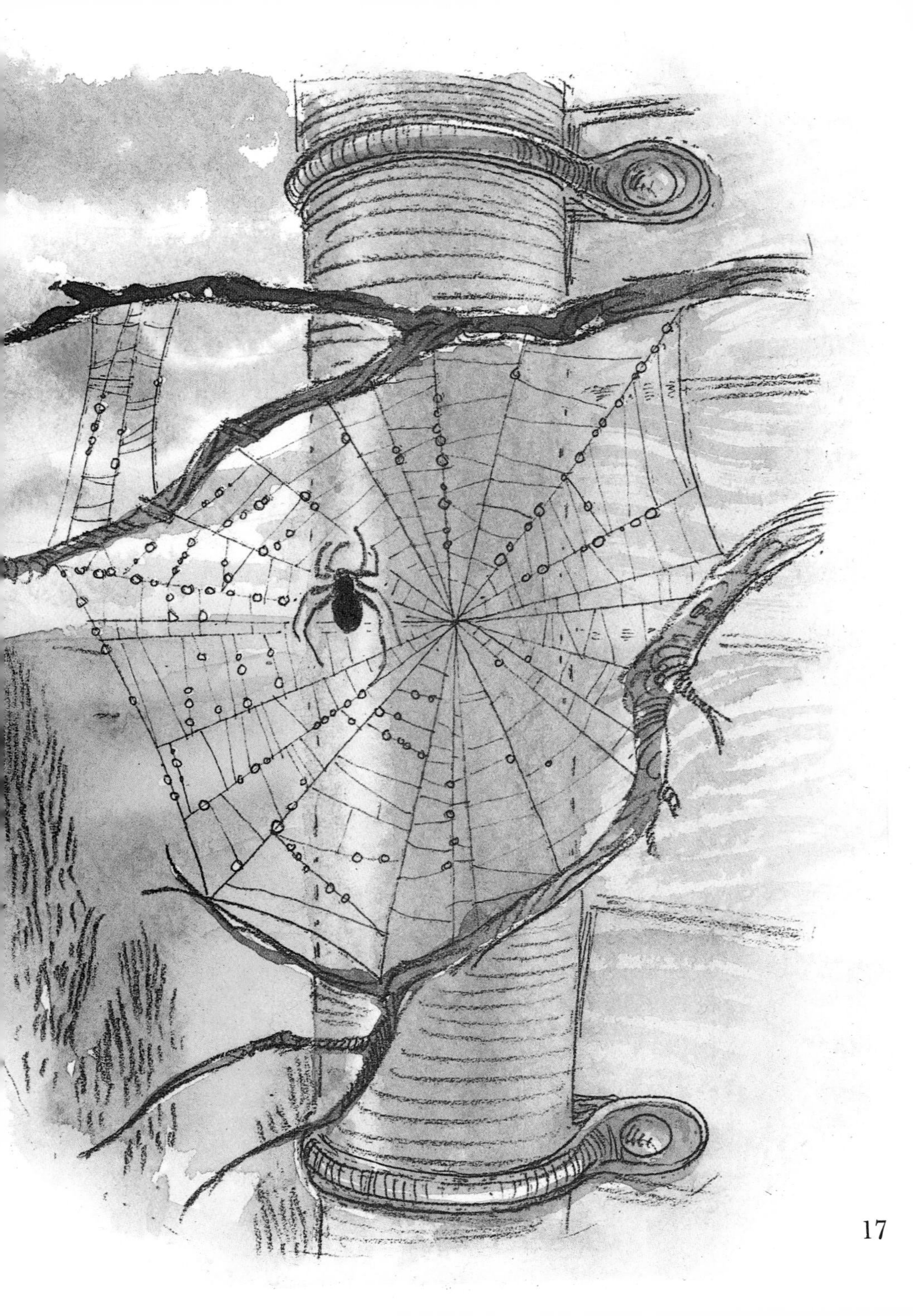

To the Rain

Rain, rain, go away,
  Come again another day,
Little Johnny wants to play.

It's raining, it's pouring,
  The old man's snoring;
He got into bed
  And bumped his head
And couldn't get up in the morning.

Rain, rain, go to Spain,
  Never show your face again.

A Sunshiny Shower

A sunshiny shower
Won't last half an hour.

On the First of March

On the first of March
  The crows begin to search;
By the first of April
  They are sitting still;
By the first of May
  They've all flown away,
Coming greedy back again
  With October's wind and rain.

One Misty, Moisty Morning

One misty, moisty morning,
  When cloudy was the weather,
I chanced to meet an old man
  Clothed all in leather;
Clothed all in leather,
  With a strap beneath his chin.
How do you do, and how do you do,
  And how do you do again?

From January to December

January brings the snow,
Makes our feet and fingers glow.

February brings the rain
Thaws the frozen lake again.

March brings breezes loud and shrill,
Stirs the dancing daffodil.

April brings the primrose sweet,
Scatters daisies at our feet.

May brings flocks of pretty lambs,
Skipping by their fleecy dams.

June brings tulips, lilies, roses,
Fills the children's hands with posies.

Hot July brings cooling showers,
Apricots and gillyflowers.

August brings the sheaves of corn,
Then the harvest home is borne.

Clear September brings blue skies,
Goldenrod, and apple pies.

Fresh October brings the pheasant,
Then to gather nuts is pleasant.

Dull November brings the blast,
Makes the leaves go whirling fast.

Chill December brings the sleet,
Blazing fire and Christmas treat.

Observation

Rain before seven,
  Fine before eleven.
When the dew is on the grass,
  Rain will never come to pass.

Red sky at night,
  Shepherd's delight;
Red sky in the morning,
  Shepherd's warning.

March winds and April showers
  Bring forth May flowers.

When the clouds are upon the hills,
  They'll come down by the mills.

Cuckoo, Cherry Tree

Cuckoo, cuckoo, cherry tree,
  Catch a bird, and give it me;
Let the tree be high or low,
  Let it hail or rain or snow.

Evening Red and Morning Gray,

Evening red and morning gray,
Send the traveler on his way;
Evening gray and morning red,
Bring the rain upon his head.

If All the Seas Were One Sea

If all the seas were one sea, What a *great* sea that would be!
If all the trees were one tree, What a *great* tree that would be!
And if all the axes were one axe, What a *great* axe that would be!
And if all the men were one man, What a *great* man that would be!

And if the *great* man took the *great* axe,
And cut down the *great* tree,
And let it fall into the *great* sea,
What a splish-splash that would be!

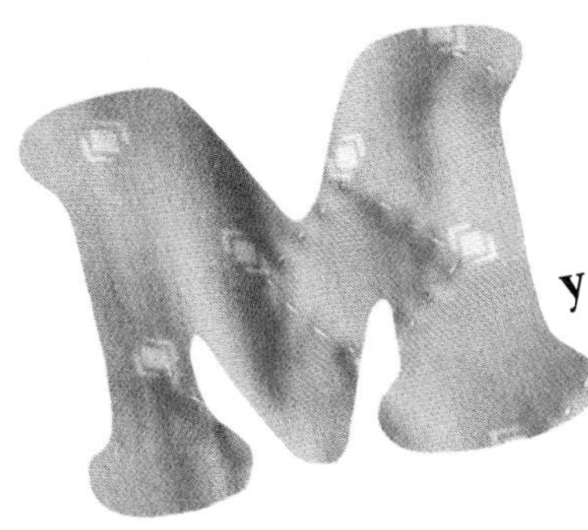

My Lady Wind

My Lady Wind, my Lady Wind,
Went round about the house, to find
A chink to get her foot in;
She tried the keyhole in the door,
She tried the crevice in the floor,
And drove the chimney soot in.

And then one night when it was dark,
She blew up such a tiny spark,
That all the house was pothered;
From it she raised up such a flame,
As flamed away to Belting Lane,
And White Cross folks were smothered.

And thus when once, my little dears,
A whisper reaches itching ears,—
The same will come, you'll find,—
Take my advice, restrain your tongue,
Remember what old nurse has sung
Of busy Lady Wind.

The North Wind

The north wind doth blow,
And we shall have snow,
And what will poor Robin do then?
Poor thing.

He'll sit in a barn,
And keep himself warm,
And hide his head under his wing,
Poor thing.

The Winds

Mister East gave a feast;
Mister North laid the cloth;
Mister West did his best;
Mister South burnt his mouth
Eating cold potato.

Blow, Wind, Blow

Blow, wind, blow!
And go, mill, go!
That the miller may grind his corn;
That the baker may take it,
And into bread make it,
And bring us a loaf in the morn.

When the Wind Blows

When the wind blows,
Then the mill goes;
When the wind drops,
Then the mill stops.

There Was an Old Woman

There was an old woman tossed up in a basket,
Ninety times as high as the moon;
And where she was going, I couldn't but ask it,
For in her hand she carried a broom.

"Old woman, old woman, old woman," quoth I,
"O whither, O whither, O whither so high?"
"To sweep the cobwebs off the sky!"
"Shall I go with you?" "Ay, by-and-by."

Hush-a-Bye, Baby

Hush-a-Bye, baby, on the tree top,

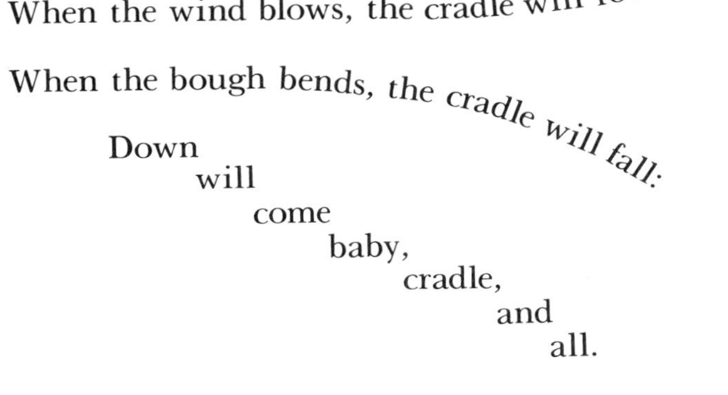

When the wind blows, the cradle will rock;

When the bough bends, the cradle will fall;

Down
will
come
baby,
cradle,
and
all.

Hey Diddle, Diddle

Hey diddle, diddle,
The cat and the fiddle,
The cow jumped over the moon;
The little dog laughed
To see such sport,
And the dish ran away with the spoon.

The Man in the Moon

The man in the moon
Came down too soon,
And asked his way to Norwich;
He went by the south,
And burnt his mouth
With supping cold plum porridge.

The Balloon

"What is the news of the day,
Good neighbor, I pray?"

"They say the balloon is gone up to the moon!"

Bedtime

The Man in the Moon
Looked out of the moon,
Looked out of the moon and said,
" 'Tis time for all children on the earth
To think about getting to bed!"